A TWEEN GIRL'S GUIDE TO PUBERTY

Love and Celebrate Your Changing Body

The Complete Body and Mind
Handbook for Young Girls

Abby Swift

BEMBERTON
BOOKS

SOMETHING
FOR YOU

Thanks for buying this book. To show our appreciation, here's a **FREE** printable copy of the "Life Skills for Tweens Workbook"

WITH OVER 80 **FUN ACTIVITIES JUST FOR TWEENS!**

Scan the code to download your FREE printable copy

TABLE OF CONTENTS

INTRODUCTION

Welcome to puberty!

Puberty is an important time in your life. It is a sign that you are growing into a young woman, and your body is changing from a child to an adult. While puberty is something to look forward to, it can sometimes be a little overwhelming. Your body is about to undergo many changes — some may have already begun! During this time, you might feel uncertain about how to handle those changes and what to expect in the future. But don't worry! This book is here to help you understand what puberty is, why it happens, and how it affects your body.

Puberty is described as "the process of physical maturation where an adolescent reaches sexual maturity and becomes capable of reproduction" (Breehl & Caban, 2023). While it may sound complicated, puberty is pretty simple to understand. During puberty, your body prepares for the possibility of having a baby, which means you can become pregnant. For a woman to become pregnant and have a child, certain hormones and traits are required. As you enter puberty, your body begins to release the necessary hormones to make pregnancy possible.

Puberty marks your body's preparation for the possibility of having a baby, and one of the most significant changes it includes is having your first period. Many cultures celebrate a girl's first menstrual cycle as a symbol of her transition into womanhood. While puberty can sometimes feel a little scary, it is the world's most natural and common experience. Did you know that there are more women than men on Earth? That means that many young girls around the world are going through puberty, just like you, and can relate to the same emotions you may be experiencing. Always remember, you are not alone on this journey.

Boys also go through puberty. While their journey isn't exactly the same as yours, they also experience changes as their hormones cause them to grow and develop into men. Puberty is a time full of transformations and new experiences, and the more you understand it, the easier it will be to navigate the changes happening to your body. This knowledge can also help you support your friends who may be feeling uncertain about their changing bodies, just like you.

What Will I Learn in This Book?

As your mind and body undergo so many changes during puberty, it is natural to have questions. And that's where this book comes in — it will help answer those questions! Inside, you'll learn about the physical and emotional changes you experience during puberty, such as changes in your body shape, your breasts growing bigger, and hair growing in new places.

You'll also learn about your first period, including what it is, how to prepare for it, and what you should expect when it arrives. And let's not forget about the exciting milestone of choosing and buying your first bra! We'll help you navigate the process and find the prettiest and most comfortable bra.

Personal hygiene becomes more important as you enter puberty. We'll cover topics like getting enough sleep, taking care of your skin, using deodorant, and everything you need to know about looking after your changing body. Additionally, we'll look into friendships and the importance of building and managing them during puberty. This includes managing strong emotions, handling conflict better, and building lasting relationships.

But most importantly, this book will show you that you are unique. Out of 7.8 billion people in the world, there is only one of you. Your body and mind are capable of so many incredible things, and together, they shape the person you are. This book will help you better understand how to love and appreciate your body and boost your self-confidence. Your body is beautiful, strong, and capable of achieving many wonderful things.

Finally, as you enter puberty, you might start feeling differently about people, and that's completely normal. But it is crucial to understand how to navigate your emotions and relationships. Eventually, you may even develop romantic feelings for someone. Knowing what to expect and how to manage those feelings is essential when that happens.

Why Should I Read This Book?

As you can see, many things happen and change during puberty. It's normal for you to have questions about puberty and what to expect in the coming years. This book will provide you with answers to many of these questions.

In today's world, social media has many ideas about puberty and how it "should" be. Still, it's important to remember that every girl is unique. That means your puberty journey will be unique to you. You may experience puberty earlier or later than your friends, and this can sometimes make you worry that something is wrong—especially if you read conflicting advice online. But not everything you read online is true or applicable to your experience. The truth is puberty is a unique and personal journey. Everyone is different, and what you experience is normal and natural.

By reading this book, you will understand why your experience with puberty may differ from that of your friends. You'll learn how to navigate your changing emotions, friendships, and relationships as you enter puberty. This book will also equip you with the necessary skills to mature into an adult and help you manage all the changes you will go through.

The primary purpose of this book is to help girls in the same position as you understand their growing and changing bodies. By the end of this book, you'll understand how puberty works, how your body changes during this phase, and why it's essential to love and celebrate your body just the way it is. Are you ready to go on this journey of self-discovery, learning to love yourself and care for your growing body? Let's get started!

1

EMBRACING YOUR CHANGING BODY

*"Womanhood is a whole different thing from girlhood.
Girlhood is a gift...womanhood is a choice."*
~ Tori Amos

Puberty is an exciting time in a girl's life, and knowing what is happening to your body will help you feel prepared for when it starts happening to you. If you notice significant changes occurring in your own body or the bodies of your friends, it is a sign that you (or they) have entered puberty.

During this time, you may also begin to feel different and more emotional compared to before. Some girls may experience these emotional changes earlier than others, while others may not experience as many emotional changes. But rest assured, it's all a normal part of puberty. So, what is puberty anyway, and why does it happen?

Understanding Puberty: What's Happening, Inside and Out?

Lots of changes occur when you enter puberty. These changes include sudden growth spurts, changing body shape, and growing hair in new places. But that doesn't fully explain what is happening to your body and why. To help you understand puberty and embrace your changing body, you must first learn what puberty is.

What Is Puberty, and When Does It Start?

Puberty is the period in your life where your body starts changing to reach sexual maturation. That means that your body becomes capable of having a baby. Your body changes from a child to an adult — even if you are still a child when it happens. These changes are caused by a hormone released by your brain when you reach a certain age ("Everything You Wanted To Know About Puberty," n.d.).

What Are Hormones?

Hormones are chemical messengers that your brain and other organs release to make things happen in your body (Mandal, 2022). Hormones are usually secreted by your brain and travel through your bloodstream to reach your organs and other body parts. In the case of puberty, hormones are secreted from your brain, pituitary glands, and ovaries. They relay messages to the rest of your body, such as your sex organs, signaling to them that it is time to change and mature.

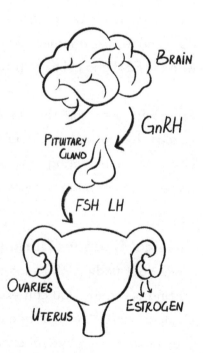

The hormone that your brain releases is called the gonadotropin-re-leasing hormone (GnRH). GnRH travels to your pituitary gland (also in your brain) and then through your bloodstream. When the pituitary gland receives the GnRH, it releases two other hormones: follicle-stimulating hormone (FSH) and luteinizing hormone (LH). These hormones are responsible for most of the changes in your body.

FSH, LH, and GnRH travel through your bloodstream to your ovaries. Your ovaries are in your lower abdomen and form a part of your sex organs. They contain all the eggs that can be used to make a baby when you get pregnant. Additionally, your ovaries also produce and release another hormone called estrogen. Estrogen works with the FSH and LH to help your body reach sexual maturity.

These hormones work together to help your body mature and cause various physical and emotional changes. Let's explore some of these changes, remembering that everyone is unique, so your physical and emotional changes might differ from your friends.

Physical Changes During Puberty

Since your body is changing from a child to an adult capable of getting pregnant, you can expect many physical changes. These changes won't happen all at once. Instead, they will occur gradually over time. Some physical changes may start earlier than others. Here are some of the physical changes you may experience during puberty:

- Sudden growth spurts (suddenly getting taller).

- Changes in your body shape. You may get wider hips, a curvier figure, or bigger breasts.

- Skin changes. You might start getting more pimples or acne.

- Stronger body odor. Your body odor may smell stronger, and you might sweat more.

- Hair growth. You will notice hair growing in new places, and the hair you already have might become darker.

This book teaches you how to manage these physical changes and embrace your changing body. Remember that puberty is a normal part of growing up and is experienced by everyone on Earth, men and women alike. So, you are definitely not alone in this journey.

Emotional Changes During Puberty

According to Planned Parenthood ("Puberty," n.d.), the hormones that cause all of these physical changes in your body also trigger emotional changes. When you enter puberty, you may experience your emotions more intensely. This can include happiness, excitement, frustration, anger, and sadness. While not all of these emotions are always positive, they are entirely normal. It will take time for your body and mind to adjust to these hormones, which can result in challenging emotions.

Sometimes, you might not even understand why you feel how you feel. Don't worry — these feelings result from the hormones in your body. They will come and go, and as you get older, your body will adjust to the hormones, resulting in less frequent intense emotions. Later in this book, you will learn how to manage your emotions effectively.

When Does Puberty Typically Start?

Puberty usually begins between the ages of 8 and 14 in girls. However, it's important to note that some girls enter puberty a bit earlier or later than this. In addition, not all the physical changes will occur simultaneously. In fact, you may experience some changes, such as changes in your body shape and skin condition, before others. While your first period usually indicates that you have entered puberty, other signs may come beforehand.

As mentioned earlier, every girl is unique, and so is her body. You may start puberty earlier or later than some of your friends, and that's completely normal. If you notice your friends are going through puberty, you can support them by being an understanding friend. This will make the entire process much easier.

What About Boys? Do They Also Experience Puberty?

While boys don't have periods like girls do, they do go through puberty. Boys typically go through puberty between the ages of 8 and 14, although it's common for boys to start puberty a bit later than girls. Similar to girls, there are many physical and emotional changes in boys during puberty. These changes include:

- Sudden growth spurts.

- Their voices get deeper.

- They develop stronger body odor.

- The possibility of acne.

- Hair growth on the face, genitals, and under the arms.

- Their sex organs (testicles and penis) grow bigger.

Boys, like girls, also experience stronger emotions due to hormonal changes during puberty. This can sometimes affect their behavior. Again, it's important to remember that puberty in boys is entirely normal, and the timing of these changes may vary by individual.

Growth Spurts and Body Shape: Celebrating Your Unique Figure

One of the changes you experience when entering puberty is growth spurts. A growth spurt is when you suddenly gain height or weight (Growth spurts & baby growth spurts, 2021). While you usually grow steadily for most of your life until you reach adulthood, you grow a lot faster in a short period when you are a baby, and when you enter puberty. In addition, during puberty, some parts of your body may grow even faster than others. In boys, you may notice that their arms and legs grow faster than the rest of their bodies.

But why do growth spurts happen when you enter puberty? Just like all the other changes in your body, growth spurts happen because of your hormones. The same hormones that cause your breasts and eggs to develop will cause other body parts to grow quickly.

You will also see changes in your body shape. For example, you may notice that your hips become wider, your legs and bottom become bigger, and your breasts grow. However, that isn't always the case. Some girls are naturally curvier than others, and everybody is unique and beautiful in their own way. Some girls may have larger breasts and hips, while others don't experience significant changes during puberty.

Just because you don't experience many physical changes during puberty doesn't mean something is wrong. Since your body is unique, it might not develop in the same way as those of other girls. Many girls have similar body shapes to their mothers. So, if your mother is curvier, your body shape might also be curvier. If your mother is slimmer, you might also have a slimmer figure.

The beauty of genetics, which includes the physical, intellectual, and emotional traits you get from your parents and grandparents, is that it makes you unique. You are a combination of your parents, but you are also your own person. That means that you develop at your own pace. Whether you experience growth spurts at 8, 14, 16, or never at all, it is entirely normal. There is no right or wrong way to enter and experience puberty.

Instead of comparing yourself to your friends and classmates, you should focus on celebrating your unique body shape and growth spurts. Remember that your body is strong, capable, and beautiful. It will enable you to do many great things, including having children, if and when you are ready.

Hair, There, and Everywhere: The lowdown on Body Hair

Body hair is natural — everyone has it. Some people have more body hair than others, and some people's body hair might also be darker. But no matter who you are, you will develop more body hair as you enter puberty. The same hormones that cause your body to change and let you experience stronger emotions also increase your hair growth. You may notice more hair growing in these areas:

- On your legs.

- Under your arms.

- On your face (on your lip and brows).

- On your labia and pubic bone (pubic hair).

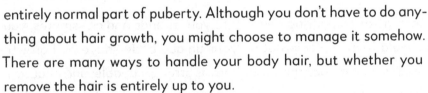

Additionally, the hair you already have on your body might become darker. This is an entirely normal part of puberty. Although you don't have to do anything about hair growth, you might choose to manage it somehow. There are many ways to handle your body hair, but whether you remove the hair is entirely up to you.

How to Handle Body Hair

There are several methods for managing and reducing body hair. However, it's important to remember you don't have to remove any hair if you don't want to. If you keep your body hair, maintaining your personal hygiene is still essential. This includes keeping the area where the hair grows clean.

If you want to remove your body hair, exploring the various hair-removal options is helpful. Here are five methods you can consider.

SHAVING

Expense:
$ $

Difficulty:

Hair regrowth time:
A few days

How it works:
Cuts it off near the skin

Which Body parts :
Legs, underarms, bikini area
(with caution)

There is a chance of nicking yourself with the blade, and the hair may grow back thicker and darker. Avoid using it on your face. Some people get rashes from shaving.

TRIMMING

Expense:
$

Difficulty:

Hair regrowth time:
A few days

How it works:
Cuts it off (not as close to the skin as shaving)

Which Body parts :
Legs, underarms, pubic hairs

Cautionary note:
Trimming is not suitable for very short hairs on the face and legs.

WAXING

Expense:
$ $ $

Difficulty:

Hair regrowth time:
A few weeks

How it works:
Plucks it from its root beneath the skin

Which Body parts :
Anywhere

Cautionary note:
Use caution when using wax at home to avoid skin damage or burns.

HAIR REMOVAL CREAM

Expense:
$ $

Difficulty:

Hair regrowth time:
A few days

How it works:
Dissolves the hair

Which Body parts :
Anywhere but your intimate areas

Cautionary note:
Some people may develop a reaction to the hair removal cream as it is a chemical.

LASER HAIR REMOVAL

Expense:
$ $ $ $ $

Difficulty:

Hair regrowth time:
Months or years; sometimes never

How it works:
Dissolves the hair from the root to the tip.

Which Body parts :
Anywhere

Cautionary note:
At-home laser hair removers are available, but therapists administer the most effective treatments during multiple sessions.

Other options for hair removal include threading and sugar waxing, each with their own pros and cons. If you want to remove some body hair, it is worth exploring your options and trying different hair removal methods to find the best option. Remember, what works for one person might not work for another, and what works on one part of your body might not work on every part.

Hair Removal Is Not Necessary!

While you may consider some of the hair-removal options above, it's important to know that you don't have to remove any hair you don't want to. Body hair is completely normal, and there is no reason to remove it if you don't wish to do so. However, even if you don't want to remove any hair, it's still important to keep it healthy.

Grooming your body hair involves keeping it clean and dry. Washing the area regularly with warm water and soap and applying deodorant to your underarms will help keep your body hair in good condition. Remember, removing body hair in some places while leaving it in others is perfectly acceptable. How you choose to manage your body hair is entirely up to you. Do whatever makes you feel comfortable and confident.

Key Takeaways from Chapter 1

- Puberty is the process of your body maturing from a child to an adult, triggered by hormones released by your brain.

- During puberty, you will experience numerous physical and emotional changes. These include shifts in body shape, breast growth, and changes in your skin. You may also feel your emotions more intensely.

- Boys also go through puberty, although the signs and changes they experience may differ. Hormones play a significant role in puberty for both boys and girls. Puberty typically begins between the ages of 8 and 14 for both girls and boys.

- Puberty brings about growth spurts, where your body shape may change, and your breasts will grow and develop. Remember, regardless of how your body changes, it is unique, beautiful, and deserving of celebration.

- When entering puberty, you will also notice hair growing in new places, including under your arms, on your legs, and in the genital area. This hair growth is normal. You can leave it as is or use one of many hair-removal methods. It's important to know that there is nothing wrong with body hair, and removing it is a personal preference.

Getting your first period is one of the significant signs of puberty. While your first period may feel new and unfamiliar, there is no need to worry — it's an entirely natural process. In the next chapter, we will discuss everything you should know about your first period and every period after that.

YOUR FIRST PERIOD—
A RITE OF PASSAGE

One of the changes your body goes through during puberty is that you start getting your period. When you experience your first period, it can feel unfamiliar and might be a little intimidating, especially if you aren't prepared for it. However, just as going through puberty is a natural part of life, so is having your period. In this chapter, you will learn everything you need to know about your first period to help you prepare for it and celebrate this milestone when it occurs.

Understanding Periods

If you understand what is happening in your body, your first period won't feel nearly as confusing. As discussed in the previous chapter, your body changes from a child to a woman during puberty. One aspect of being a woman is the possibility of getting pregnant and having babies someday. Consequently, every month, your body prepares for the possibility of conception. It releases an egg from your ovaries that travels to your uterus, where it waits to be fertilized by a sperm cell.

If your egg is fertilized by a sperm cell (which can happen if you have sex), the egg attaches to your uterus, and a fetus starts to grow. This fertilized egg needs a lot of nutrients to grow and develop. These nutrients come from your blood. Every month, your uterus produces a thick lining of blood to support the growth of a possible fetus.

However, if your egg is not fertilized by a sperm cell, it does not attach to your uterine lining. In this case, the thick blood lining detaches from your uterus and exits your body through your vagina. This process is called a period — when the blood and tissue from your uterus come out of your body. Several hormones, such as estrogen, progesterone, and FSH, control your menstrual cycle. Your brain controls these hormone levels, which fluctuate throughout the month, ultimately resulting in your period if fertilization does not occur.

While your first period can be confusing, there is nothing to worry about. The blood discharged from your uterus through your vagina doesn't mean you are injured. Instead, it is part of the uterine lining in your womb that is no longer needed by your body. Even though it looks like a lot of blood, the blood cells in period blood are already dead and won't be missed.

While it might look like you are losing a lot of blood, most girls typically lose only two or three tablespoons of blood during their period ("Heavy Menstrual Bleeding," 2022). Some girls might lose a little more, and others a little less. This is known as having a heavy or a light period. Both variations are normal and depend on the size of your uterus and the thickness of the lining.

How Long Does a Period Last?

Your menstrual cycle is typically 28 days long. This cycle consists of four phases: the menstrual phase, the follicular phase, the ovulation phase, and the luteal phase ("Menstrual Cycle," 2022).

The menstrual phase marks the beginning of your menstrual cycle and starts on the first day of your period. Generally, periods last between four and seven days but can vary in duration. After your period ends, your body enters its *follicular phase*. During this phase, one of your ovaries develops an egg that it will eventually release for possible fertilization. This process takes approximately 14 days. Around the 14th day of your cycle, the mature egg is released from the ovary. This is known as the *ovulation phase*. The egg then travels through the fallopian tube to the uterus, awaiting possible fertilization. This is known as the *luteal phase*.

During the follicular, ovulation, and luteal phases, your uterus is hard at work producing a nutrient-rich, blood-filled lining to support a fertilized egg. If the egg is not fertilized, it will trigger your next period when it reaches the uterus.

While a typical menstrual cycle takes around 28 days, many factors influence the actual length of your cycle. Some people have longer menstrual cycles, while others have shorter ones. Both variations are entirely normal. When you start having your period, it may be less regular, and the cycles may vary in length. Sometimes, they may be longer than 28 days; other times, they may be shorter. This is normal as your body matures and adjusts to the hormones. As your body changes, your periods will become more regular.

Period Basics: What to Expect and How to Prepare

As you get older and your periods become more regular, you will better understand how and when to prepare for them. However, your periods will likely be less predictable when you enter puberty. One month, you might have a very light period or just a bit of spotting. Spotting is when you see a little bit of blood, but it's not enough to require a pad or tampon to absorb. It's just a few spots of blood. Spotting also sometimes occurs between periods and is normal when you first enter puberty and have your first periods.

The following month, you may have a heavy period that lasts longer. There's no need to worry. Your body will adjust, and your periods will become more predictable as you mature. However, being prepared and knowing which signs to look out for can help you manage your period better.

For many girls, periods usually start between ages 8 and 14. But again, because your body is so unique, your period may start slightly earlier or later than that. A few days before your period starts, you may notice some changes. Many girls experience mood changes, such as sadness or irritability, before and during their periods. This is due to the hormonal changes in the body. Some girls also notice more pimples or acne just before their periods start.

You may also experience cramps in your lower abdomen. For some women, these cramps are pretty light and hardly noticeable, while others have cramps that cause discomfort that disrupts their day. These cramps occur because the muscles in the uterus contract to expel the blood lining. In addition to menstrual cramps, you may also experience a sharp pain in your abdomen, which might feel like a pain in your fallopian tubes or ovaries. And you may also experience discomfort in your lower back.

Thankfully, there are many remedies for period pain. Heat pads, such as warm beanbags or hot water bottles, work wonderfully to reduce menstrual cramps and reduce back pain. Over-the-counter pain medication can also help to relieve these symptoms. In addition, light exercise, such as walking or running, can help reduce cramping and menstrual discomfort (McCallum, 2021).

When your period begins, you may notice that the color of the blood is brown or dark red. It may then change to bright red for a few days before switching back to brown before ending. This color variation is normal as the brown blood is older. Most women experience their heaviest flow during the first two days of their periods. However, this can change as your period becomes more regular. Some women may not experience these symptoms, and their period produces the same flow throughout.

Your period symptoms might differ from those around you, but that does not mean anything is wrong with any of you. Every girl's period journey is different and unique. Initially, when your period first starts, you may experience a mix of symptoms as your body adjusts to the hormonal changes. Over time, however, you will learn to better predict your period and be more prepared for it. Of course, you will also need the right products to manage your period.

Period Products: Finding What Works Best for You

When managing your period, you will need to choose from various period products available on the market. Each product has advantages and disadvantages, so determining which ones work best depends entirely on your needs and preferences. It may help to try a few products before deciding which one you prefer. Here are five period products you can consider.

Pads

Pads are one of the oldest period products available. They are made of cotton or absorbent material and are attached to your underwear. When the blood comes out of your vagina, it is absorbed by the pad, which prevents it from staining your underwear or clothes.

Pads are easy to use and are relatively inexpensive. However, they cannot be worn when swimming, as they won't stick to a wet bathing suit and will also absorb the water. There is also a risk of leakage if they shift out of place. Unfortunately, most disposable pads contribute to plastic pollution, although some environmentally friendly reusable pads are now available.

Tampons

Tampons also absorb blood. However, unlike a pad that sits in the underwear, a tampon is inserted into the vagina to absorb it before it exits the body. Using a tampon is relatively easy. It has a string that hangs outside of the body, and the tampon is removed by pulling on the string.

Tampons are smaller and more compact than pads and can be worn when swimming and doing other sports activities, but they are more expensive than pads and require some practice to use correctly.

Environmentally friendly tampons with biodegradable packaging are available to reduce plastic pollution.

Applicator Tampons

Applicator tampons work just like regular tampons, but come with a long dispenser made of plastic that makes inserting them into the vagina easier than a regular tampon.

They are more expensive than pads and regular tampons and contribute to plastic pollution if they have a plastic applicator. However, many applicator tampons are now made with cardboard applicators, which are kinder to the environment.

Menstrual Cups

Menstrual cups have gained popularity in recent years. They are small, round cups made from medical-grade silicone. The cup is folded and inserted into the vagina, where it collects the blood. The cup must be removed and emptied regularly before reinserting.

Menstrual cups can be used for up to five years, making them cost-effective and environmentally friendly. They can be worn during any activity and don't require frequent changes like tampons or pads. However, using a menstrual cup requires practice, as there are different shapes, sizes, and firmness levels to consider.

Menstrual Discs

Menstrual discs are similar to menstrual cups. However, whereas a menstrual cup is inserted into the vaginal canal, a menstrual disc is inserted deeper into the vagina, below the cervix. They offer similar advantages, including being more environmentally friendly than pads or tampons. However, using menstrual discs correctly without spilling blood may take some practice, and they don't last as long as menstrual cups.

Regardless of the period products you choose to use, there are some things to remember when it's that time of the month.

Tips for Using Period Products

When you first start having your period, learning how to use each period product can be challenging. Since you have to replace the products often, you may wonder what you should do with the used products. Here are some essential tips:

Tips

- **Replace your period product every 6–8 hours to avoid leakage.** Pads, tampons, menstrual cups, and discs can only handle limited volumes of blood, so they must be changed regularly. If your pad or tampon is at capacity, it is time to swap it out.

- **Do not flush period products down the toilet.** Period products can block the drains. Wrap them in toilet paper or put them in a small bag and dispose of them in the trash.

- **Wash your hands before and after changing your period products.**

- **Keep a few extra products with you, just in case.** Having a few extra products is always recommended to use or share with a friend.

- **One size does not fit all!** There are different sizes for each period product, based on the size of your vagina and the heaviness of your flow. Choose the right size and absorbency level for your body and flow to ensure comfort and minimize period pain.

- **Don't be embarrassed to ask for help when you need it.** Learning to use period products can be daunting, but remember that you aren't alone. Every woman on Earth knows what a period is and how it feels, so don't hesitate to ask your parents or trusted adults if you have questions or need help.

Remember, every woman goes through this experience, and there is no need to be embarrassed or afraid to seek assistance when needed.

Period Positivity: Embracing Your Menstrual Cycle

"Society has placed a taboo surrounding periods and menstrual health, as if we should be ashamed of this natural and miraculous process that ultimately keeps the human species alive."
~ Tracy Lockwood

While having your first period can be scary, it is also a special moment worth celebrating. It's a sign that you are growing into a woman, and one day you might have the incredible ability to bring new life into the world (if that's what you choose).

Getting your period is a significant step in your journey to becoming a woman. It means your body is preparing for the remarkable ability to create and nurture life. The hormones driving your period and puberty also play a crucial role in shaping you into a strong and extraordinary individual. It's essential to embrace and value these changes as symbols of the amazing person you're becoming.

For a long time, society made people feel that periods were not something to be discussed. Thankfully, times have changed, and many people are challenging that perspective. There's absolutely nothing to be ashamed of when it comes to your period. Whether you get it earlier or later than your friends, whether your flow is light or heavy, and whether you choose to use pads, tampons, menstrual cups, or discs, it's all a normal part of being a woman.

In many cultures around the world, a girl's first period is celebrated with elaborate ceremonies. It might be time to introduce this tradition to your own period celebration. Why not have a period party when you get your first period? You can eat cake, watch your favorite movie, and celebrate this milestone with friends and family. It's time for society to start celebrating the miracle of life and everything that comes with it, including periods.

Your menstrual cycle is a part of who you are and deserves to be celebrated. Even if you don't always feel like being grateful for your period, especially when you're experiencing emotions or pain, remember that without your body, hormones, and uterus, humans wouldn't exist.

Having a period party when you get your first period is an excellent way to embrace and celebrate this wonderful milestone in your life. It can make the experience more positive for you and your friends.

Key Takeaways from Chapter 2

- Your first period can be a scary experience, but understanding what happens in your body can help you embrace it. It usually happens between 8 and 14 years old, and occurs when an unfertilized egg reaches your uterus.

- Period blood is the blood from the lining in your uterus that is expelled when the egg isn't fertilized. The muscles in the uterus contract to expel this lining, causing menstrual cramps and bleeding.

- Exercise, painkillers, and heat pads work wonderfully for reducing period pain. It's normal for some girls to experience much heavier periods and cramping than others.

- There are lots of period products you can use, including tampons (regular and applicator), pads, menstrual cups, and menstrual discs.

- Having your first period is a big milestone and deserves to be celebrated. It signifies that you are becoming a woman.

Another part of entering puberty is the growth and development of your breasts, which means it is time to buy your first bra. This is an exciting part of growing up. In the next chapter, you will learn all about buying your first bra.

FINDING THE PERFECT BRA —
A BEGINNER'S GUIDE

Owning and wearing a bra is an important step on the journey to womanhood. Unsurprisingly, many girls are excited about buying their first bra. However, as you will learn, not all bras are the same. It's important to know what to look for when buying a bra to ensure it is as comfortable and functional as possible. So, when is the right time to shop for your first bra?

When to Shop for Your First Bra

There is no right or wrong time to shop for your first bra. Some girls start wearing bras at eight, while others only need them at 14 or 15. Since everyone's body develops differently, it's natural for each person to require a bra at different times. If you feel self-conscious about your breasts, you might find a training bra  a comfortable way to ease into wearing a bra.

While there is no set time to start wearing a bra, there are signs that indicate it might be time to go shopping for your first bra. Remember that a bra is meant to support your breasts. If your breasts or nipples start feeling uncomfortable or you feel self-conscious about them (though you have no reason to — your body is beautiful just the way it is), it might be time to go bra shopping. Here are some signs that it might be time.

1. Your Breast Buds Are Developing

Breast buds are the tissue around and under your nipple that grows during puberty ("The First Bra Guide," 2019). As your breast buds develop, your breasts will start to grow, and there will be more actual breast tissue. This is a sign that your breasts are developing, and getting a bra might make you feel more comfortable. As your breast tissue develops, your breasts may feel sore or swollen. In this case, a bra can offer support and help ease any discomfort.

If you have larger breasts, a bra can provide much-needed support and reduce the strain on your lower back.

2. Your Nipples Are Sensitive or Show Through Clothing

The hormones responsible for the changes in your body, including your breasts growing, can make the nipples feel sensitive or stand upright, causing them to show through clothing. Wearing a bra with soft padding can alleviate discomfort caused by hard or sensitive nipples.

Sometimes, the nipples may also darken. This is normal, but it might cause them to show through light-colored tops. A flesh-colored bra can help prevent nipples from showing through clothing and help you feel more confident wearing any outfit.

3. You Feel More Breast Movement During Exercise

If you notice your breasts more when you exercise and feel like they are bouncing up and down, it may be time to buy a sports bra. These bras are designed to offer more support when exercising and can stop your breasts from bouncing around.

They're also important as your breasts grow to prevent sagging as you get older. Whether your breasts are small or large, wearing a sports bra during exercise becomes essential.

4. You Feel Self-Conscious About Your Breasts

If you feel self-conscious about your breasts being more noticeable in certain clothes, wearing a bra can help you feel more confident. Of course, you have absolutely no reason to feel self-conscious about your breasts — they are unique and a part of your beautiful body. But if it bothers you, a bra can help you feel more secure and confident. Wearing a pretty bra can boost your confidence and help you appreciate and love your breasts.

5. Your Friends Are Wearing Bras

While you shouldn't compare yourself to anyone else, it can feel strange when your friends are all wearing bras, but you aren't. It's fine if you want to wear a bra to fit in with your friends.

Remember that everyone develops at their own pace. Just because you don't *need* a bra now doesn't mean you won't need one later. Shopping for pretty bras with your friends can be a fun experience, so if you want to, you can buy a bra.

6. Do You Need to Wear a Bra?

While you might want to wear a bra for support, comfort, or any of the above reasons, no rule says you must wear one. Some women prefer not to wear bras, which is completely fine. While a bra offers structure and support, you can choose not to wear one.

Whether you wear a bra or not — and, if so, which type of bra you wear — is entirely up to personal preference. Determining when to wear a bra, if you want to wear one, is only half the story. The other half is deciding which type of bra is right for you. There are many different types of bras, each with their own characteristics. Learning to differentiate between these bras can help you choose the most suitable bra when shopping. Let's explore the different types of bras available.

Navigating Different Types of Bras

In addition to training and sports bras, various other kinds of bras are available. Some bras provide support, while others are designed to make the breasts look more shapely. Understanding the different types of bras can help you decide which is most suitable for you.

There are several things to look for in a bra, but most importantly, it needs to offer enough support and be comfortable. If it stabs you, pinches you, or digs in, it won't be comfortable. Finding the perfect bra can be a bit of a challenge, but it's worth the effort. Here are some different types of bras you'll come across:

Training Bras

Training bras are a common choice for girls starting out. These bras are usually made from thin cotton, making them soft, comfortable, and lightweight. Some training bras have a clasp in the back, like a regular bra, while others have a stretchy band that you can pull over your head.

Training bras don't offer much support for growing breasts, but they are perfect for girls whose breasts have just started developing or who have

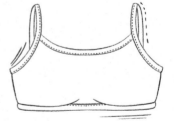

sensitive breasts and nipples. Training bras help you get used to the feel of wearing a bra.

Bralettes

Bralettes are similar to training bras, but sometimes have soft padding, as well. They often have a clasp at the back, like a regular bra, and can be made from cotton, stretchy fabric, or lace. They also help cover the nipples to prevent them from showing through a shirt.

Like training bras, they don't offer much support, but they are extremely comfortable. While training bras are usually for girls just entering puberty, bralettes are available to anyone. Many women who don't need additional support from their bras prefer bralettes because they are lightweight and comfortable.

Soft-Padded Bras

Soft-padded bras have more structure than bralettes and training bras. These bras have a thicker, sometimes removable cup that fits over the breast. These cups help to give breasts

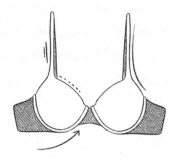

a rounder appearance and prevent nipples from showing through clothing. They usually have a clasp in the back and can have thick or thin straps.

Because of their comfort and support, soft-padded bras are one of the most popular bras.

Push-Up Bras

Push-up bras look similar to soft-pad-ded bras, but their cups have different inside designs. These cups often have a wave pattern on the bottom, with slightly thicker padding. Push-up bras are meant to push your breasts up and make them look bigger.

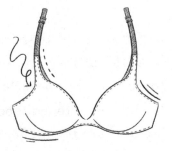

However, push-up bras don't offer more support than soft-padded bras. Women usually wear them because they like how they make their breasts look. When you first enter puberty, your breasts may not be big enough for a push-up bra, as there needs to be enough breast tissue to push up. But if you like the look of these bras, they can be something you look forward to buying when you are a bit older.

Underwire Bras

Underwire bras look like soft-padded bras, but they have a wire running along the bottom seam of the bra. This wire gives the bra more structure and support, especially for larger breasts. Some people prefer underwire bras, as they can provide more support. However, 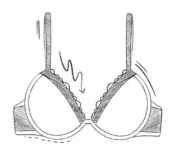 it's a personal preference, as others find the wire uncomfortable, especially when worn for long periods.

Some underwire bras also have padding or push-up padding. If you buy an underwire bra, it's crucial to ensure it fits properly. Otherwise, the wire may dig into your skin and be uncomfortable.

Sports Bras

Sports bras are just as popular as soft-padded bras and are worn by most women when exercising. Sports bras are designed to fit tightly and offer more support. They are specially designed to support breasts during vigorous exercise and protect them from bouncing up and down.

Regardless of how large your breasts are, it is recommended to wear a sports bra while exercising for maximum support. If you notice your breasts moving around a lot when you're active, a sports bra might be the best option as a first bra. That being said, it's important to know that sports bras are designed to be functional rather than to look nice.

Now that you know about the different types of bras available, it's important to understand how to find a bra that fits you correctly. If the bra doesn't fit properly, it can soon become uncomfortable and may not provide the necessary support.

Getting the Right Fit: Tips and Tricks

When buying your first bra, the priority is getting the fit right. There are many different styles of bras available, but it's all about getting the one that is perfect for you and your individual body.

Getting a bra that fits correctly will help you feel comfortable and give your growing breasts the best support. But how can you tell if a bra fits correctly? First, let's consider some signs that indicate a bra does not fit right.

How to Tell If a Bra Doesn't Fit Right

There are a couple of things to consider when trying on a bra. If the bra does not fit correctly, it will become uncomfortable throughout the day and may not offer the right support. These are common signs that a bra doesn't fit well:

Tips

- The straps dig into your skin or fall off your shoulders.

- The band around your body rides up in the front or back.

- The bra's wire or band digs into your ribs.

- The bra's band is too loose; you can easily pull it away from your body.

- Your breasts spill over the bra's cups.

- The bra cups gape away from your body.

If you notice any of these signs, it means the bra doesn't fit you properly. While you might not consider these big issues initially, they can become problematic when you wear the bra for a long time. Remember that you will be wearing a bra for most of the day, every day. So, if it doesn't fit properly in the store, it won't fit properly at home, either. Wearing a bra that is too small or too big is like wearing shoes that don't fit you properly: The longer you wear them, the more uncomfortable they become.

Measuring Your Bra Size

The best way to ensure your bra fits you properly is to get measured for your correct bra size. Although you can try on bras in the store to see if they fit, having your measurements will help you determine which size bras to try. This is especially important when shopping for bras online since you can't exchange them easily. So, how do you measure your bra size?

Bra sizes work differently than other clothing sizes. A bra usually has two indicators of size: a number and a letter. The number represents the band size, while the letter is the cup size. For example, a 30A means the band size is 27 inches, and the cup measurement is one inch bigger than your band measurement. It may sound complicated, but it is pretty straightforward once you know how to measure your bra size. So, let's see how to determine your bra size.

Measuring Your Band Size

Measuring your bra band size is simple. Place a measuring tape around your ribs, right under your breasts. Ensure the measuring tape is level all around your body. Then, write down the number of inches your body measures around. It will be much easier if someone helps you to measure your band size, as they can ensure the measurement is accurate.

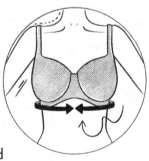

Measuring Your Cup Size

To measure your cup size, take the measuring tape and run it across your body, with the tape lying across the fullest part of your breast. It's best to do this while wearing a non-padded bra. Again, ensure the measuring tape is level to get an accurate measurement.

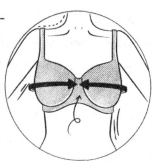

Determining Your Bra Size

Once you have these measurements, you can get your bra size. The band size comes first. Add 3 inches to your first measurement to determine your band size. For example, if your band measurement is 27 inches, you'll need a size 30 bra. If your result is an odd number,

Measurements	Bra Sizes
27 in.	30
28 - 29 in.	32
30 - 31 in.	34
32 - 33 in.	36
34 - 35 in.	38
36 - 37 in.	40

you will want to go up to the next size. For example, if your measurement is 28, 28+3=31, round up to a 32 band size. Take a look at the chart to help you determine your bra's band size based on your measurement.

To find your cup size, you need to subtract the measurement of your band size from the measurement of your breast size. For example, if your breast measurement is 33 inches and your band measurement is 30 inches, you would do the following: $33 - 30 = 3$. This means that your bra cup size is

Difference Between Measurements	Bra Cup Size
< 1 in.	AA
1 in.	A
2 in.	B
3 in.	C
4 in.	D
5 in.	DD/E

a C. Here is another table to help you determine your cup size.

You can use these numbers to determine your bra size. For example, if your band measurement is 29 inches and the difference between your breast and band measurement is 2 inches, your bra size is 32B. Knowing your bra size can make it easier to find bras that are suitable for you.

If you're unsure about measuring your bra size at home, you can also have it professionally measured at a clothing store. Many stores offer this service for free to help their customers find the perfect bra. If you feel more comfortable, you can ask a friend or family member like your mom, aunt, or sister, to measure their bra size with you. Once you know your bra size, you can focus on finding the right type of bra that suits your needs.

Key Takeaways from Chapter 3

- Buying your first bra is an exciting experience. There are so many bras to choose from; the best bra for you depends on your needs and the level of support you want.

- There is no right or wrong time to buy a bra. If your breasts start to grow, your nipples are visible through your clothes, your breasts are sensitive, or you notice them moving more when you exercise, it might be a good time to consider getting your first bra.

- There are various types of bras, including training, bralettes, soft-padded, push-up, underwire, and sports bras. Each has unique functions. Choosing the right bra is all about personal comfort and finding what works best for you.

- Measuring your bra size is essential to ensure a proper fit, which is crucial for comfort and support. Taking accurate measurements can help you find the perfect bra size for your body, making it easier to find the right bra.

As you enter puberty, along with choosing your first bra, it's time to adopt a fresh approach to your personal hygiene and skin care. In the next chapter, we will consider the importance of personal hygiene during this stage of your life and provide practical tips to help you develop effective routines.

PERSONAL HYGIENE —
TAKING CARE OF YOUR
GROWING BODY

As you start puberty, you will notice many changes in your body. In the previous chapters, you learned that these changes are a result of the hormones released by your brain, which help your body mature. However, these same hormones also affect your body odor, the amount of sweat you produce, hair growth, and your skin. This chapter will explore how to manage these effects with good hygiene.

The Importance of Personal Hygiene

Before puberty, your daily routine was more straightforward. You didn't have to worry about body odor, sweating, hair removal, or your period. But all of that changes when you enter puberty. Developing a more detailed daily personal hygiene routine is essential to ensure you care for yourself properly.

Personal hygiene means caring for your body and keeping it clean — and it's crucial for everyone. The habits you put in place now will likely be with you for the rest of your life. Establishing an easy-to-follow and complete personal hygiene regimen now will save you a lot of time and make you feel more confident throughout the day.

A good personal hygiene regimen can boost your confidence by ensuring you are well cared for. It also helps improve your mental health and reduces stress, which is good for your well-being. For example, by showering daily and using deodorant, you can be sure that you smell nice, which boosts your self-confidence and reduces stress.

Maintaining good personal hygiene also ensures you are physically healthy. Showering, brushing your teeth, and washing your hands all help keep your body healthy and protect you against germs. This helps prevent you from getting sick, which most people want to avoid.

As you can see, personal hygiene is essential for many reasons — but what exactly does it entail, and how do you keep your body clean?

Skincare: Tackling Acne and Developing a Routine

One important aspect of personal hygiene is caring for your skin — especially your face. The hormonal changes during puberty often affect your skin, making it oilier, which can lead to pimples, acne, and breakouts. Even girls with non-oily skin experience breakouts, especially before and during their periods. Increased acne and pimples are normal during puberty but usually clear up as you get older.

That said, following a simple skincare routine can greatly help your skin. A daily skincare routine helps keep your skin clean, moisturized, and protected from the sun. It can also help prevent acne and breakouts and reduce the chances of acne scars.

A skincare routine doesn't have to be complicated. You don't need expensive products that celebrities and influencers often promote. You simply need a cleanser (or gentle face wash), moisturizer, and sunscreen to keep your skin clean and healthy. Using these products daily will significantly help your skin.

A morning and evening skincare routine also helps you focus on keeping your skin clean and healthy. It also gives you time to relax and focus on caring for yourself, which is crucial for your mental health. This is why it is a good idea to set aside time for your daily skincare routine each morning and evening.

If you wear makeup, you should remove it before starting your skincare routine. Use a makeup-removing wipe, micellar water, or a gentle makeup-removing oil to lift all the makeup from your skin.

Then, wash your face with warm water and a mild, oil-reducing cleanser or face wash. Gently pat your skin dry with a soft towel, then apply a light moisturizer to keep your skin soft and glowing. Finally, don't forget to apply sunscreen. Using sunscreen daily can prevent wrinkles and protect your skin from sun damage as you get older.

It's also important to clean your face at night to remove all the dirt and sweat from your day. Wash your face again with a mild cleanser and use a moisturizer. You don't need sunscreen at night.

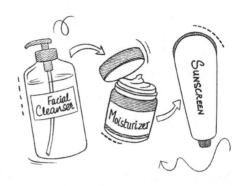

The Importance of Dental Hygiene

Looking after your teeth is equally important. By the time you start puberty, you have likely lost most of your baby teeth, so the teeth you have now are the ones you will have for the rest of your life. If you don't care for your adult teeth and gums, you may get cavities, which is a painful and unpleasant experience requiring a trip to the dentist.

Practicing good dental hygiene is vital. Brush your teeth twice a day with a soft toothbrush and toothpaste to keep your teeth and mouth healthy. Regular flossing also helps prevent the development of cavities and ensures your mouth is clean and fresh. Clean teeth also help keep your breath fresh, boosting your self-confidence.

Avoid eating too many sugary foods or soft drinks, as the sugars in them harm your teeth. And, if you can, it's a great idea to go to the dentist once a year for a checkup to ensure your teeth are healthy. By following basic dental hygiene practices, you can maintain a healthy smile!

Showering, Deodorant, and More: Keeping Fresh and Clean

Another essential aspect of good personal hygiene is showering every day (or every other day, if you have sensitive skin). As mentioned earlier, the hormones during puberty cause you to sweat more, which leads to body odor.

Body odor occurs when sweat combines with the trillions of bacteria naturally present on your skin. When sweat comes into contact with the bacteria, it mixes with the fats and salts and can produce an odor. Not all body odors are the same — some may be unpleasant, while others don't smell at all.

Fortunately, there is an easy solution to combat body odor. Showering daily and using deodorant can help reduce sweating and prevent unpleasant odors. Additionally, washing your clothes regularly and wearing clean clothes can help reduce odors, since your clothes absorb sweat and can start to smell if not washed.

Of course, there might be days when you need to shower more than once. For example, a shower after sports practice or a visit to the gym can help you smell clean and fresh.

Applying deodorant after a shower and in the morning before getting dressed can also help control sweat and body odor throughout the day. There are various types of deodorant available, including:

- Deodorant sprays

- Deodorant sticks

- Roll-on deodorants

- Gel deodorants

- Antiperspirant deodorants (which block pores to reduce sweating)

- Natural deodorants made with ingredients like baking powder, coconut oil, and essential oils. These are environmentally friendly and don't contain aluminum, which may be harmful to your body. Natural deodorants may not prevent sweating entirely, but they prevent sweat from smelling.

You can use whichever deodorant you prefer to help you feel clean, fresh, and confident.

Hair Care: Keeping Your Locks Clean and Healthy

Caring for your hair is as important as keeping your body clean during puberty. When you enter puberty, changes in your hormones can affect your hair. It may become oilier at certain times of the month, or your scalp might become dry and flaky. That's why using the right hair products for your hair type is crucial to keep it clean and healthy.

You don't have to wash your hair every day, unless it becomes very oily or dirty. How frequently you wash your hair depends on your hair type and how active you are. For instance, if you exercise regularly, your hair may become greasy. Pay attention to the condition of your hair to determine how often it needs washing.

Understanding the changes in your hair during puberty and using the proper hair-care routine can keep your hair looking and feeling its best.

Overall, good personal hygiene helps improve your health and confidence. When you are clean and well-maintained, you will feel more energetic, confident, and self-assured. You may also find that people around you treat you with more respect.

As you enter puberty, it becomes clear that personal hygiene is vital, and these habits will remain essential throughout your life. However, caring for your growing body extends beyond personal hygiene and cleanliness. So, what else can you do to practice self-care during puberty?

Exercise and Sleep: Prioritizing Your Well-Being

Getting enough sleep is cru-cial, especially during puberty. Your body needs enough rest to develop properly. Lack of sleep can affect your mood, attention span, and school per-formance (Jitesh et al., 2021). As a tween, you should aim for at least seven or eight hours of sleep per night.

Sleep is crucial for your health and well-being. While your body rests when you sleep, your brain is hard at work, releasing hormones and chemicals. These substances need time to work their magic. Furthermore, getting enough sleep will help you feel more energized during the day.

So, how can you get a good night's sleep? Here are some tips that can help you fall asleep faster and get a good night's rest:

- **Give yourself enough time to rest.** Aim for seven to eight hours of sleep.

- **Maintain a regular sleep schedule.** Try to go to bed and wake up at the same time each day.

- **Reduce caffeine intake in the daytime.** Highly caffeinated drinks, like coffee and energy drinks, take up to 12 hours to go through your body and can negatively affect your sleep.

- **Keep your room dark, quiet, and cool.** Cover any flashing lights (such as computer lights), as they can disrupt sleep.

- **Avoid using screens or tablets at least one hour before bedtime.**

- **Turn screens off and make your bedroom a "no charge zone!"** Avoid charging or keeping screens in your room, as they can distract and wake you up.

- **Exercise in the daytime.** Regular exercise can help you sleep better.

The Importance of Eating Well

Eating a healthy diet during puberty can also benefit your overall well-being. Did you know sugary foods and preservatives can affect your skin and health? Eating too many sugary and processed foods can lead to oilier skin and more breakouts. Additionally, the preservatives in junk food can disrupt your hormones, contributing to acne and mood swings.

Drinking water and staying hydrated is another crucial aspect of managing your personal hygiene. Water makes up 60 percent of your body, and not drinking enough can negatively affect your body and mental health. Drinking water and being properly hydrated can improve your skin, energize you, and help reduce period pain and discomfort. Teenage girls should drink at least six to eight glasses of water a day. If you exercise, you may need to drink more to replace the water lost through sweating.

Healthy foods like fresh fruits and vegetables are rich in antioxidants, vitamins, and minerals. These nutrients are essential for growth, development, regulating hormones, and improving mental health. Eating a nutritious diet also enhances your physical health, which is vital during your teenage years.

THE IMPORTANCE OF REGULAR EXERCISE

Exercise is beneficial for your physical health and plays a significant role in your mental well-being. Exercise releases endorphins, sometimes called your body's "happy hormones." These endorphins increase your energy levels and improve your mood. Exercise also reduces cortisol, the stress hormone, which helps to reduce feelings of stress and anxiety.

To keep your heart and body healthy, doctors recommend doing at least 30 minutes of exercise a day.

What kinds of exercise can you do? There are many types of exercise you can enjoy. You can go for a walk (like walking to school or walking your dog), participate in a team sport at school, or go for a cardio class at the gym. The specific type of exercise isn't as important as keeping your body active and moving.

If you find exercising challenging, ask a friend to join you. A workout buddy can make exercise more enjoyable and feel less like work. Whatever you do, get out there and exercise. It is so important for everyone to exercise. Just remember the many benefits for your health, including improved mood, increased energy levels, and better sleep.

 Key Takeaways from Chapter 4

- Caring for your growing body becomes even more important when you enter puberty. This includes practicing good personal hygiene to ensure you are healthy.

- Personal hygiene involves various aspects, such as showering regularly, keeping your hair, teeth, and nails clean, getting enough sleep, and regular exercise.

- Hormonal changes during puberty can lead to acne and breakouts. A daily skincare routine can help prevent breakouts, keep your skin clean and fresh, and boost self-confidence.

- Dental hygiene is crucial as your adult teeth replace your baby teeth. Brush your teeth twice a day, floss regularly, and visit the dentist for checkups.

- Maintaining personal cleanliness, such as showering, using deodorant, washing your hair, and keeping your nails short and clean, can increase your confidence and protect against germs. It's important to shower daily and use deodorant to combat sweat and odor.

- Getting sufficient sleep is crucial, especially during puberty. Your body needs sleep to grow and regulate your hormones.

- Regular exercise is important during puberty. It can improve self-confidence while also reducing period pain. Aim for at least 30 minutes of exercise each day.

- Eating a healthy diet and staying hydrated by drinking enough water both contribute to improved skin, balanced hormones, and a better mood.

By practicing good personal hygiene, prioritizing sleep, exercising regularly, and maintaining a healthy diet, you can be sure you are taking good care of your body during puberty. These healthy habits will set you up for success as a teen and later in life.

The next chapter will discuss everything you should know about cultivating friendships during puberty. By following the proper steps, you can develop strong friendships that last a lifetime.

5

CULTIVATING FRIENDSHIPS

As you grow up and get older, you may notice that your friendships start changing, too. When you were younger, it was easier to make friends. You likely had girlfriends and boyfriends, and all played together without a problem. As you get older and develop more of your own interests, your friendships might also start changing.

Managing your changing friendships is an important part of growing up. It's crucial that your friends positively impact your life. Good friends should build you up, encourage you, and support you.

Building lasting friendships can be challenging in today's world, but in this chapter, you will learn how to navigate these changes and cultivate new friendships.

The Changing Landscape of Tween Friendships

As you already know, you can expect many physical and emotional changes when you enter puberty. The emotional changes you experience when you enter puberty can affect how you feel about those around you and how they feel about you.

As you get older, your interests also change. You may become more interested in a specific sport, instrument, subject, or after-school activity. You will meet new people who share these interests, and you might become closer friends with them. At the same time, your older friends will develop their own interests, and you may grow apart.

Changing schools can also lead to losing contact with older friends and making new ones. It's a natural part of growing up to lose touch with older friends and make new ones who share your interests. But just because you don't have shared interests with someone doesn't mean you can't be friends with them.

Even if you and your best friend have different interests, you can continue to be friends while making time for your own pastimes. As you make new friends, your best friend will too, and it's essential to give each other room to grow. This can help bring you closer together as friends and help you make even more friends.

During puberty, it's common for relationships with your male friends to go through changes. Just as hormonal changes affect your body, they can also affect how you perceive people, including boys. This is true for boys, as well. Sometimes, boys you used to be friends with might start acting differently, and you might develop different feelings toward them.

These changes are a normal part of growing up and discovering new emotions. It can be challenging to navigate friendships, especially when everyone has entered puberty and is undergoing physical changes. However, understanding how to manage your relationships and respecting the differences between you and your friends can help build stronger friendships.

Eventually, things tend to settle down as everyone adjusts to the new hormonal changes. Therefore, it's essential to keep your friendships as strong as possible. Try not to burn bridges or end friendships with people you might want to reconnect with later. While you may experience ups and downs in your relationships, it's crucial to have a core group of friends who can support each other through the challenges of puberty.

Sometimes, your friends might be mean to you or reject your friendship. In such cases, it's okay to step away from those friendships. Remember, you are fantastic and deserve friends who love and respect you. If your current friends don't treat you well, it's time to look for new ones.

Conflict is an unavoidable part of life, and learning how to manage it is important. No matter how hard you try, you won't always be able to avoid conflict. In those situations, it is crucial to learn how to react to and manage conflict without losing control of your emotions. So, how should you navigate conflict as a teenager or adult?

Navigating Conflict: How to Handle Disagreements

Conflicts and disagreements are a normal part of life. During the tween and teen years, it's common to experience sensitivity to certain emotions. You may feel more self-conscious or insecure, leading to strong emotional reactions to situations. Additionally, you may feel misunderstood, which can lead to conflicts with parents, siblings, or friends.

This heightened sensitivity may be due to hormonal changes, but could also be due to greater pressure to perform well at school, in your sport, and at home. You are growing up and will naturally have more responsibilities, and these heightened feelings of responsibility might cause more conflicts.

While it's normal to feel upset sometimes, and your feelings are entirely valid, knowing how to navigate conflict is essential. If you let your emotions escalate, you may do or say things you later regret.

By staying in control of your emotions, you can calmly navigate conflicts and find ways to peacefully resolve them. Harshita Makvana (2023) from Mom Junction shares these 10 steps to navigate and resolve disputes as a teenager. Following these steps will help you navigate conflict and remain in control of your emotions:

· Step back and consider the other person's perspective. Try to see the situation through their eyes.

· Carefully listen to what the other person is saying, especially when they talk about how something makes them feel. Don't interrupt them when they share their feelings.

- Share your feelings. Be honest and keep calm to help them understand your perspective.

- Don't let your emotions overwhelm you. Take deep breaths when you feel like you are getting too emotional.

- Avoid digging up past conflicts. Resist the temptation to say, "You always do this," as that won't help resolve a dispute. Instead, focus on discussing the current conflict and finding a resolution.

- Try to find a solution that respects both of your opinions. Aim for a solution that serves both of you.

- Learn to compromise. The solution might not give you precisely what you want, but it's important that both you and the other person are satisfied.

- Learn to say sorry. It can be difficult to admit when you've made a mistake. However, learning to acknowledge and apologize for your mistakes can help immensely in a conflict situation. People always appreciate a sincere and honest apology.

- If you cannot find a solution, it might be necessary to bring in a mediator. A mediator is a person who isn't on anyone's side. They are neutral and are there to listen to both parties and help find a solution.

- Accept the other person's apology. Holding a grudge won't make you feel better, and resolving the conflict is more important than who is right.

Staying calm and listening to another person shows maturity. Remember the saying, "You have a choice between being right and being happy." Sometimes, it's more important to be the bigger person and accept an apology than to prove that you're right and they are wrong.

Compromising and navigating conflicts positively doesn't mean you're a pushover. It demonstrates maturity by prioritizing your friendships over the need to always be right.

That's not to say you shouldn't stand up for yourself. If someone crosses a line or hurts your feelings, you need to tell them. This shows them that their words or actions are unacceptable and helps define your boundaries. Standing up for yourself and addressing inappropriate behavior helps cultivate self-respect and the respect of others.

Building Strong and Supportive Friendships: Creating Lasting Bonds

The goal of conflict resolution is to keep your relationships with your friends and family healthy. But another important part of being a teenager is building new relationships and strengthening the ones you already have. As we have already discussed, as you grow up, your interests will change — and so will the things you need from your friends.

Since we all have different person-alities, we look for different things in our friends. For example, if you're shy, an outgoing friend can help you feel more comfortable in new situations. If you love sports, hav-ing friends who share this interest can give you more to talk about and opportunities to support each other.

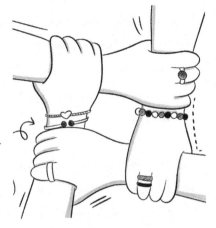

Unlike family, you can choose your friends. The good friends you surround yourself with in school are the ones who will inspire and motivate you to achieve your goals, study hard, and be successful. These friends will also love and support you and your changing body during puberty.

Choosing supportive friends at school who truly want the best for you can help make you happier and more successful. But to *have* a good friend, you must also *be* a good friend. So, how can you build strong and supportive friendships?

Building Positive Friendships

Navigating strong emotions can be tricky during puberty. Your hor-mones might cause you to overreact sometimes, and even though that's normal, it can put pressure on friendships. The key is building strong relationships based on trust and understanding, where you and your friends feel loved and supported. So, how can you achieve this? Here are some tips:

Top Tips for Building Positive Friendships

- Respect your friends and their differences. Their differences make them unique, and that's why they are your friends.

- Be honest with your friends. Tell them how you feel and let them help you. And if they hurt or upset you, tell them.

- Protect your friends. Stand up for them when they aren't around, and never gossip about them behind their backs.

- Always make time for your friends. Neglecting them can make them feel like you don't care, and that can drive you apart. So, make time for them, especially when they need you.

- When your friend tells you a secret—keep it! One of the easiest ways to ruin a friendship is to betray a friend's trust. So if your friend tells you something in confidence, keep it to yourself.

- Give your friend space to grow. Just as you will grow and develop new interests, so will your friends.

- Support and encourage your friends to help them reach their goals. You expect your friends to support you, so do the same for them.

QUALITY OVER QUANTITY

If there's one thing you should remember about friendships as you grow up, it's that quality is always better than quantity. When you were younger, you probably had many friends. But as you get older, you realize that not everyone who is friendly with you is your friend.

Having one or two close friends who support and encourage you and who are always there for you is better than having thousands of friends on social media.

Your priorities change. Instead of having many friends to play with, you need friends you can trust to keep your secrets and stand up for you, even when you're not there. That's why choosing your friends carefully becomes more important as you get older.

Social Media: Friend or Foe?

Social media has become an important part of our lives, influencing friendships positively and negatively. We spend a lot of time on social media, liking posts, sharing with friends, and exploring new interests. But social media isn't always positive for friendships, and it's important to use it mindfully. Here are some pros and cons to consider.

Using Social Media To Build Friendships

It allows you to communicate with your friends when you're not together. Platforms like WhatsApp, Instagram, and Twitter all have chat options to check in with your friends and keep in touch.

You can meet new friends who share your interests. You can join groups or communities to connect with like-minded people.

PROS

You can share photos and videos with friends, letting them know you're thinking of them even when apart.

You can share photos, videos, and information about things you love, which can help you make even more friends.

Social media can create pressure to fit in or do things you're not comfortable with, this is called peer pressure. For example, if your friend keeps sending you pictures of piercings and urging you to get one, you might feel pressured to do it. Remember, it's okay to make decisions based on what feels right for you.

People can act differently online. Sometimes, people are braver behind a screen and may say mean things, pick fights, or hurt others' feelings. But remember just because it's a text, doesn't make the words any less hurtful.

CONS

Cyberbullying is a real problem. Posting mean comments online is a form of cyberbullying, and it can cause a lot of hurtful feelings. Always think before you post.

It's always there. Once something is posted on social media, it's always there. Meaning it's available for everyone to see for ever. So before you post something ask yourself: "Would I be happy if this is always there for everyone to see?"

Key Takeaways from Chapter 5

- Friendships change as you get older. As you develop new interests, you'll make new friends. Some old friendships may fade, while new ones will form.

- Learning how to navigate and resolve conflicts is crucial. Everyone faces conflicts in their lives, and it's important to learn how to handle them with care and respect.

- As you grow up, you'll realize that having a few true friends is more important than many superficial ones. To have loving and supportive friends, always be a loving and supportive friend in return.

- Social media can be both positive and negative for friendships. Learn to use it safely and responsibly. and always consider your friend's feelings before putting something out there.

We've already explored the effects of puberty on your emotional well-being in this book, but now it's time to learn how you can control and manage your feelings. In the next chapter, you will learn about embracing and managing your changing emotions during puberty.

EMBRACING YOUR EMOTIONS — NAVIGATING MOOD SWINGS

During puberty, along with the physical changes you experience, you'll also notice some emotional changes. Understanding and navigating these emotional shifts is vital for your health and well-being. While these new emotions and mood swings are perfectly normal, they can cause challenges in your relationships if not managed effectively.

Managing your emotions and recognizing your mood swings before they occur is an important part of growing up. In this chapter, we'll focus on discovering why you sometimes have mood swings, which emotions you may experience, and how you can manage your emotions using helpful coping strategies. But first, what causes all these emotions and mood swings? Let's take a look.

Understanding the Connection Between Hormones and Emotions

As mentioned before, your brain and body produce more hormones during puberty. These include an increase in estrogen, progesterone, FSH, and LH, which are responsible for your body's physical changes. Some of these hormones (specifically estrogen) can affect your body's serotonin levels (Tallman Smith, 2017).

Serotonin is a chemical messenger that sends signals from your brain to the rest of your body and plays a role in many functions, like digestion, sleep, and mood. During your menstrual cycle, your body produces varying levels of estrogen. And just before your period, those estrogen levels fluctuate dramatically. Many scientists believe that your estrogen levels are linked to your serotonin levels. Some say that an increase in estrogen leads to a decrease in serotonin, which could cause sudden mood changes (Tallman Smith, 2017).

As a result, these hormonal changes can affect how your brain works and how you feel. Because of this, it's common for girls to experience mood swings before and during their periods. It's important to know that these mood changes are normal. In fact, research shows that most women — approximately 90 percent — experience mood swings throughout their menstrual cycles (Holland, 2019).

WHAT ARE MOOD SWINGS?

Just like the weather can change throughout the day, your moods can also change during your menstrual cycle. These sudden mood changes are called mood swings, and they happen because of the changing levels of hormones in your body.

From the outside, it might seem like your mood suddenly changed for no apparent reason. The good news is that most, if not all, women experience mood swings during their menstrual cycles. This means that most women will understand when you have these sudden mood swings.

Of course, it's important to remember that sudden mood swings do not excuse bad manners or behavior. Later in this chapter, we will look at coping strategies for managing mood swings.

Although hormone fluctuations play a significant role, they aren't the only reason you may experience mood swings.

OTHER FACTORS THAT CAUSE MOOD SWINGS

Several other factors might also contribute to mood swings. These factors can be made worse by fluctuating hormones, making the mood swings more intense and frequent. Here are some additional factors that can contribute to mood swings:

· Stress

· Too little sleep

· Caffeine consumption

· Eating highly processed and sugary foods

Fortunately, you can help manage and reduce your mood swings by addressing the factors contributing to them. We'll discuss these factors in a later section. However, before we do that, it's important to identify and understand the range of emotions you may experience during your menstrual cycle and which emotions are intensified by hormonal fluctuations.

Identifying Emotions

Emotions are a natural part of life. As you grow up, you'll notice they become more complicated and difficult to understand. When you were younger, emotions were pretty straightforward and easy to understand. If someone took your toy, you might have felt angry. If you fell in the playground, you probably felt sad. And you likely felt happy when something good happened, like your mom buying you an ice cream. But, as you get older, your emotions and how you express them become more complex.

Everyone experiences emotions differently. Some people cry when they're angry, happy, or tired, while others laugh when they are cross or become quiet when they're sad. As your emotions become increasingly influenced by hormonal changes during puberty, it's important to recognize and understand what you are feeling. This can help you manage your feelings and understand why you feel the way you do.

So, what do the different emotions feel like during puberty? Let's explore some common emotions and how they often present, which can help you better understand and make sense of your feelings.

ANGER AND IRRITATION

Anger is an emotion many women feel when their serotonin levels drop. Serotonin contributes to feelings of joy and happiness, so low levels can lead to anger or irritation. If you find that you are suddenly irritated with your friends

ANGER & IRRITATION

and family for no reason, or you get angry with them even if they haven't done anything wrong, it may be due to hormonal fluctuations in your body.

Anger often results from frustration or feeling like you are being treated unfairly, and irritation can arise from being distracted or bothered by something. However, when your anger and frustration result from hormonal changes, it's important to remember it's not necessarily someone else's fault. It's normal to feel angry or irritated, even when your hormones cause these emotions. But it's important to manage these emotions, especially when they're influenced by hormones, as the person you feel irritated or angry with may not understand what they did to deserve such a reaction.

SADNESS

Sadness is another common emotion many women experience before or during their periods. When you feel sad, you may cry or feel a sense of heartache, even if no one has physically or emotionally hurt you. Sadness is a natural part of life, and although it's not enjoyable, it's important to acknowledge and try to understand your sadness.

Sadness affects people in different ways. Some people release their sadness by crying, while others bottle up their sadness and pretend nothing is wrong. Feeling sad due to hormonal changes can be frustrating, because  sometimes you may not even know why you are feeling sad. It could be triggered by something as simple as seeing a dog on the street, or you might wake up feeling sad for no obvious reason. Remember, sadness is a completely normal emotion. Although you'll likely want to overcome your sadness, allowing yourself to experience and feel these different emotions is important.

Sensitivity

Many women feel more sensitive before and during their periods. Mood swings often cause sensitivity because you may not understand why you feel the way you do. For example, if you wake up feeling sad or angry, even when nothing has happened to make you feel that way,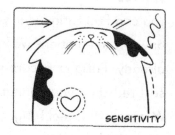

you may also feel more sensitive because you don't understand the reasons for your emotions. Sensitivity is a perfectly normal emotion, even if it can be frustrating.

When you go from feeling happy to sad to angry to tired in a short time, you may also feel more sensitive because you may not know what's causing these emotions and why they change so often. Additionally, suppose you struggle to make simple decisions, like what to do, eat, or watch. In that case, you might feel extra sensitive, especially when someone gets annoyed that you can't make up your mind.

Knowing what causes your moods and indecisiveness might help you feel less sensitive. When your sensitivity is caused by your hormones, even knowing what is causing it might not make you feel better. Still, it might help you understand why you feel the way you do.

Fatigue

You can feel fatigued if you experience any of the emotions we have discussed already. Fatigue occurs when you are so tired that you cannot think clearly. Women often feel fatigued during their periods, as their bodies are doing a lot of

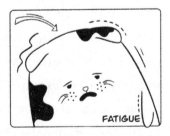

FATIGUE

extra work to expel the uterine lining. Taking frequent naps, feeling too tired to do anything, and feeling physically and mentally exhausted are all signs of fatigue.

Unfortunately, because your fatigue stems from hormonal changes, sleeping more won't necessarily make you feel better. Still, giving your body more time to rest might help with your mood swings.

Self-Consciousness

When you are self-conscious, you feel that other people are staring at you or judging you for certain things, such as how you look, dress, speak, etc. Many girls feel self-conscious when they first start puberty, and many women feel self-conscious during their periods.

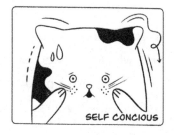

Being self-conscious can also make you feel scared to do things. For example, you might not want to go to school during your first period because you think your friends will make fun of you. But self-consciousness is often a feeling we only have about ourselves — it isn't necessarily how others feel about us.

Many people are also self-conscious about their bodies. For example, you might feel self-conscious when your hair is a bit messy, or when you feel like you look tired. Being self-conscious is a normal feeling, but it can increase just before your period.

Recognizing that your self-consciousness might be because of your fluctuating hormones can help you ignore these feelings and focus on embracing your beautiful body instead.

Recognizing and understanding your emotions is an important first step to managing them. While all emotions and feelings are normal, learning how to manage them is a crucial part of growing up.

If you cannot manage your emotions, they might start to control you, which can lead to unpleasant experiences. Fortunately, there are several proven ways to help manage emotions, enabling you to feel more like yourself both before and during your period.

Coping Strategies for Managing Mood Swings

Although the mood swings you experience before and during your period are completely normal, it doesn't mean you should just accept them. Mood swings can make you feel miserable and might lead you to be mean toward others when they don't deserve it. If you learn how to manage your mood swings, you can avoid hurting other people's feelings, improve your mood, and make your period a much more enjoyable experience. So, how can you manage your mood swings?

Get Enough Sleep

Getting enough sleep is important for any tween and teenager, but focusing on your sleep is even more important during your period. Because your hormones fluctuate more, your body needs more rest. Being tired can increase mood swings and negative emotions like sadness, irritability, and self-consciousness.

By getting seven to eight hours of sleep, you will feel more refreshed and energized, and more in control of your emotions. Sleep quality is important, so remember to follow the tips in Chapter 4 to help ensure you get plenty of rest during your period.

Drink More Water or Caffeine-Free Tea

Caffeinated and sugary drinks can potentially impact your mood swings. Caffeine has been associated with increased feelings of stress and anxiety, which can contribute to mood swings and affect sleeping patterns. Furthermore, research has shown that sugary drinks and foods can also cause increased anxiety and irritability (Sheehan, 2010).

Water and caffeine-free tea help you stay hydrated, which can improve your mood and overall health. All your body's cells, including those in your brain, need water to function. When fully hydrated, your brain works well and helps regulate your mood. Dehydration, on the other hand, can lead to tiredness, irritability, and a drop in concentration. Remember to drink water throughout the day to stay healthy.

Do Light to Moderate Exercise

Exercise is one of the best things you can do to stay physically and mentally fit. Research has shown that exercise can positively affect your mood by increasing dopamine and serotonin levels (Watson, 2019).

Even during your period, doing light to moderate exercise can help improve your mood. The combination of the mood-boosting chemicals and the fresh air from outdoor activity is known to improve your well-being and helps you sleep better.

Exercise also helps you think more clearly, which can help you manage your emotions a lot better. Going for a walk in the afternoon, participating in team sports, or taking a class at the gym can help improve your mood and help you manage your emotions and mood swings while on your period.

Eat Calcium-Rich Foods

Calcium is a mineral you get from eating certain foods, like milk, low-fat cheese, and leafy greens. Many studies have shown that eating calcium can help reduce fatigue and sadness during your period (Sheehan, 2010). Therefore, eating calcium-rich food can help you manage your mood swings.

It also helps you to feel better overall. Eating healthily and taking your vitamins also improves your body's immune system and energy levels, which helps to manage your hormone levels. If your hormone levels are regulated, so too are your mood swings.

Sit in the Sun

Did you know sun exposure can increase your serotonin levels? Studies have shown that sitting in the sun for just 15 minutes a day can increase your serotonin levels, which helps to improve your mood (Byzak, 2018). Sitting in the sun and getting fresh air can also help clear your mind, make you feel more positive, improve your mood, and reduce stress.

Just remember to wear sunscreen when going outside to soak up the sun's vitamin D.

Manage Your Stress

Stress management is also essential during your period. Increased stress can intensify mood swings, affect sleep, and make you feel more irritated and angrier overall. Therefore, before and during your period, it's important to focus on reducing stress.

There are many techniques for stress management, even when you are busy with exams or tests. Breathing exercises, light to moderate exercise, and a healthy diet can all reduce stress and help you manage your mood swings much better.

Speak to a Doctor or Medical Professional

Some women and tweens have a harder time managing their mood swings during their periods. Certain health conditions, such as polycystic ovary syndrome (PCOS) and thyroid conditions, can cause more significant hormonal fluctuations, leading to severe mood swings and other period complications. Women who struggle with these conditions are sometimes prescribed medication to help manage their hormone levels, which in turn helps manage their mood swings.

If you find that you struggle with severe mood swings despite following the tips above, it might benefit you to see a doctor to determine if something else is the cause of your fluctuating hormones. Fortunately, these conditions are rare and aren't common among young girls just starting their periods.

By implementing these strategies, you can effectively manage your mood swings and make your period a more enjoyable experience. Remember, it's normal to experience emotions, but learning how to navigate and manage them is an important part of growing up.

Key Takeaways from Chapter 6

- Mood swings during your menstrual cycle are caused by the fluctuation of hormones in your body. Just before your period starts, your estrogen levels spike, causing your serotonin (happy hormones) to dip, which can lead to mood swings.

- Many women feel sad, angry, irritated, sensitive, and self-conscious before and during their periods. These feelings are normal, but some strategies can help manage these mood swings.

- Strategies for managing mood swings include getting enough sleep, drinking more water, exercising, and sitting in the sun.

- Following these tips can also help you feel happier and more relaxed during your period.

One of the emotions you may feel during your period is self-consciousness. Many women struggle with this not only during their period but in general. In the next chapter, we'll look at ways to enhance self-confidence and love your body.

7

SELF-ESTEEM AND BODY IMAGE — LOVING YOURSELF INSIDE AND OUT

As you go through puberty, your body undergoes many remarkable changes that help make you wonderfully unique. It's natural to sometimes feel like you don't measure up, or have moments of self-doubt. However, it's important to remember that these thoughts don't reflect the truth.

In a world influenced by social media, prioritizing self-love and acceptance of your wonderfully unique body has never been more important. In this chapter, we will look at strategies to help you build your self-confidence and love your body.

Understanding Body Image and Self-Esteem

Before we dive into ways to manage your body image and self-esteem, it's vital that you first understand what these concepts are. Your body image and self-esteem are extremely important as you grow up, and developing a positive body image will help you immensely later in life. Your body image affects your self-esteem and confidence, so having a positive body image is crucial. But what exactly is body image?

What Is Body Image?

Your body image refers to the thoughts you have about your body. Many factors affect how you feel about your body, and your thoughts may change as you get older. Most people have both positive and negative thoughts about their bodies. They like some parts, while disliking others.

Tweens and teenagers often become more aware of their body image. Since the body changes so quickly during puberty, it's normal for your perception of your body to change during this time.

Your body image is the way you *see* your own body. However, it's important to remember that how you feel about your body may not align with the reality of how your body looks, especially if you feel insecure about certain parts. For example, if you think your arms are too big, you might always see them as larger in the mirror than they actually are.

Your body image is also influenced by how you *think* about your body. How you think about your body often affects how you see it, too. If you think your body is beautiful, you will look at it and see it as beautiful.

How you see and think about your body significantly affects how you *feel* about it, also known as your affective body image. This is one of the most important parts of your body image, as it plays a crucial role in how you treat your body, and greatly contributes to your self-esteem.

Finally, all these aspects influence how you *treat* your body. A positive body image is important, as it leads you to treat your body kindly.

Your body image can affect your self-esteem, with a positive body image improving your self-esteem and a negative body image potentially damaging it. But what exactly is self-esteem?

WHAT IS SELF-ESTEEM?

Your self-esteem is your confidence in your abilities and skills. Essentially, it's how you feel about yourself. Your body image is a part of your self-esteem, and greatly affects it.

Having good self-esteem helps you value yourself more. This is important in your daily life, enabling you to recognize and appreciate your uniqueness. It can also help you speak up when you're not being treated fairly. Therefore, having good self-esteem is crucial for your mental health and well-being.

Lots of factors influence your body image and self-esteem. Understanding these factors and learning how to manage them can greatly improve your self-esteem and confidence.

What Factors Affect Your Body Image and Self-Esteem?

Your body image and self-esteem are affected by various factors, such as media, society, and the changes that come from puberty. When you enter puberty, your body goes through many remarkable changes. It's natural to compare yourself to others, even if you may not want to. If you feel that you are progressing at a different pace than your friends, it can sometimes lead to negative feelings and affect your self-esteem.

Society and the media also affect your body image and self-esteem significantly. Society has ideas about how people should look, dress, speak, and behave, and the media shapes ideas about body image and self-esteem.

These standards change frequently, but they can significantly affect your feelings. Unfortunately, social media has a big influence, exposing teens to society's standards, whether they want to pay attention to them or not.

Furthermore, the people you hang out with and peer pressure can also affect your body image and self-esteem. Understanding how to deal with peer pressure and the influences of social media — and not allowing them to affect you — is important. But how can you effectively deal with these pressures?

Dealing with Peer Pressure and Social Media Influences

People often like to voice their opinions, even when they're not asked for. When the people around you feel like they have a say in how your body should look, it can make you feel pressured to feel or look a certain way.

Social media often showcases and celebrates what they deem to be the "perfect body." This can lead to a negative body image if your body doesn't match these unrealistic standards.

SOCIETY'S IDEAS OF THE FEMALE BODY

Society's ideas of the ideal female body are ever-changing. For instance, in the early 1900s, the "perfect female body" was considered to have an hourglass figure and a tiny waist. In the 1960s, a thick body with no curves was considered the "ideal female body." And in the 1980s, having a more athletic body was more fashionable.

As you can see, society's idea of the perfect female body is constantly changing. So, what does that mean for your body? It means that your body is perfect just the way it is. Regardless of whether you feel your body is "ideal" according to today's standards or not, it is beautiful in its own right.

Beauty comes in many forms, including different body shapes, and each form deserves to be celebrated. The beauty of your body is its uniqueness, and that is something that deserves to be celebrated.

The problem arises when people believe everything they see on social media. If you constantly see photos and videos of strong, muscular women, you may think something is wrong with your body if it doesn't look that way. But nothing could be further from the truth. You are unique and wonderful, and what you see on social media often isn't reality.

Social Media and Peer Pressure

This problem often becomes more significant when you feel pressured by your friends and peers. For example, if everyone dresses a certain way, you may feel pressured to dress that way. And if you don't look the same as your friends in similar clothes, you might start to believe that there is something wrong with your body.

However, that couldn't be further from the truth. Every body shape is beautiful and deserves to be celebrated just as it is. During puberty, your growth spurts may occur at different times from your peers. Certain parts of your body may grow before others. Your hips may become curvier before your breasts start developing, or you may have a sudden growth spurt without developing curves for a while.

None of that matters. What matters is how you feel about your changing body. Remember that your body experiences numerous changes during puberty, and what you see on the outside reflects what's happening inside. Some people may go through "awkward" body changes during puberty, where they feel unbalanced. That is entirely normal and all part of growing up.

Things About the Female Body Social Media Doesn't Show You

Instead of convincing yourself that you should look and dress a certain way, it's important to focus on all the beautiful things about your body. The images you see on social media are often edited and airbrushed to make models appear flawless. Here are some things you don't see in those edited pictures.

Stretch Marks

Stretch marks are tiny lines that appear on the skin when it stretches rapidly. They often occur during growth spurts, when you grow so fast that your skin struggles to keep up. Initially, stretch marks may be red. They may also be itchy or sore. Over time, they fade to white or silver and become less noticeable.

Some women use skin oils and lotions to reduce the visibility of stretch marks. However, they are a completely normal part of being human. Most people have them, and they can appear on any part of your body, such as your legs, stomach, breasts, and arms.

Cellulite

Like stretch marks, cellulite is another normal part of the human body. Cellulite occurs when fat pockets gather beneath the skin, resulting in a dimpled or lumpy appearance. Cellulite is extremely common, with 80–90 percent of women having cellulite on some part of their bodies ("Cellulite," 2021).

Although there are some methods to help prevent or reduce the appearance of cellulite, it can be difficult to remove once it occurs. However, there is no need to remove cellulite or feel ashamed of it, as it is an entirely normal occurrence, and most, if not all, of your friends will also have cellulite.

Acne

Many social media influencers use filters to edit out skin imperfections and wear makeup to make it look like they have perfect skin. In reality, though, acne, dark undereye circles, pigmentation (dark spots on your skin), and freckles are normal.

Every influencer you see on social media has some skin imperfections, even though they may try to hide them. However, there is no need to hide them. It's normal to have skin blemishes, acne, or other skin concerns. That's real life, but what you see on social media is often not reality. Instead of hiding these imperfections, celebrate them as a sign that your body is maturing.

Body Fat

Body fat is entirely normal, despite what social media may have you believe. Hip dips, a lower belly pouch, thicker thighs, and back fat are entirely normal. Each person's body stores fat in different places.

Your body needs some fat to protect your organs, give you energy, and regulate your body temperature. Therefore, your body will naturally hold on to some fat. Body fat is nothing to be ashamed of. Even though many influencers may pose and edit their photos to make it look like they have "perfect" bodies, they also have body fat stored somewhere — everyone does!

 Bloating

Bloating occurs when your stomach feels swollen and inflated, and is usually due to factors like diet, hormonal changes, or stress. Many women experience bloating throughout their menstrual cycles. Although few people talk about it openly on social media, bloating is a normal part of being human. It can happen to anyone, regardless of their body shape or size.

Instead of believing everything you see on social media and idolizing models and influencers as having "the perfect body," consider all the amazing things your body is capable of and love yourself just the way you are.

Building Confidence: Tips for Boosting Your Self-Esteem

Since self-esteem and body image affect your confidence, mental health, and physical health, learning some techniques for building your self-esteem is important. By doing so, you can embrace your changing body and develop a positive body image. Here are 11 tips for boosting your self-esteem and cultivating a positive body image:

1. Surround Yourself with Positive Friends

One of the best ways to improve your self-esteem and body image is to surround yourself with positive and encouraging friends. Supportive friends can share similar struggles and help you feel better when you feel down about your body, providing support and encouragement. During challenging times, having a positive support system is crucial. Friends who love and care for you can help you overcome any challenge, reminding you that you are beautiful, powerful, and perfect just the way you are.

2. Don't Compare Yourself to Others

While it can be difficult to do so, it's important to focus on yourself and avoid comparing yourself to others. Your body is as unique as your personality and will change at its own pace. If you enter puberty earlier or later than your friends, it doesn't mean anything is wrong with you. Instead, it is simply your body going through things at its own pace.

Instead of comparing yourself to others, focus on appreciating the amazing aspects of your body. Doing so will help you embrace and enjoy your body's changes.

3. Focus on Improving Yourself

Rather than comparing yourself to others, focus on improving yourself. If you recognize areas where you want to improve, such as your fitness, concentrate on your own abilities and progress. Instead of wishing that you were as fit as your friends, think about how much fitter you are now than you were when you started training.

4. Prioritize Your Health

Taking good care of your body is essential for improving self-esteem and body image. Prioritize your healthy by getting enough sleep, eating healthily, drinking plenty of water, and exercising regularly. You will appreciate it more when you take good care of your body. You will also feel more confident that you are doing everything possible to ensure your body is healthy and well cared for.

5. Celebrate Your Accomplishments

Celebrate your accomplishments, no matter how small they may seem. Whether it's reaching a fitness goal, achieving a good grade at school, or having your first period, celebrate it. Celebrating your accomplishments releases serotonin, which improves your mood, body image, and self-esteem.

6. Be Kind to Yourself

It's easy to be hard on yourself. People often do it. They criticize themselves for every failure and flaw. But doing so only decreases their self-esteem. Instead of focusing on your shortcomings, focus on your strengths.

Of course, you should also work on improving areas that need attention, but you shouldn't focus only on them. Instead of looking at your shortcomings as failures, think of them as progress, and remember that nobody is perfect.

As Oprah Winfrey wisely said, "Think about yourself as a queen. A queen is not afraid to fail. Failure is another stepping stone to greatness." View your shortcomings as stepping stones to greatness and use them to empower you to reach new heights.

7. Do What Makes You Happy

Doing activities that make you happy is a great way to boost your self-esteem and confidence. Doing something you enjoy — even if you aren't good at it — can give you a sense of achievement and satisfaction. It also helps to reduce stress, anxiety, and depression. Additionally, it releases serotonin, which helps to improve your mood and overall well-being.

8. Be a Good Friend

Being a supportive and caring friend also enhances your self-esteem. By helping your peers when they need you and offering advice and support, you'll feel more self-confident.

Knowing you are a good friend who supports others and helps them will improve your self-esteem by making you feel more worthy. Showing appreciation for your friends, even if you have only one or two, is essential in fostering positive relationships.

9. Tell Yourself That You Are Beautiful

Start your day by reminding yourself of all the fantastic things you can do. Repeat positive affirmations to yourself, like "I am beautiful just as I am." These affirmations gradually build a positive self-image and improve self-esteem. The more you tell yourself these positive messages, the more you will believe in your own beauty. Eventually, these positive messages will help you disregard any criticism.

10. Avoid Negative Self-Talk

No matter how demotivated you feel, never speak negatively about yourself. Negative self-talk can affect your self-esteem and body image even when meant as a joke. Focus on building yourself up rather than tearing yourself down.

11. Remind Yourself of Things You Are Grateful For

It's natural to for people to get stuck on their shortcomings or the things they don't like about themselves. However, adopting a more positive outlook, such as focusing on what you are grateful for, can greatly improve your confidence.

Be thankful for your strong and healthy body and remind yourself of this fact whenever you feel negative, and you will begin to feel more positive. Remember, you have many reasons to be grateful. Focusing on them can help boost your confidence.

By implementing these tips, you can shift your focus toward self-acceptance, self-appreciation, and self-love. Embrace your unique body and recognize the incredible capabilities it possesses. Building a positive body image and self-esteem will contribute to your overall confidence, well-being, and happiness.

Key Takeaways from Chapter 7

- Your body image is how you think about, feel about, and see your body. It is often influenced by your peers, social media, and society. Developing a positive body image is crucial for improving your self-esteem and self-worth.

- Your self-esteem is how you feel about yourself and your abilities. Having a positive body image helps improve your self-esteem.

- Social media often paints an unrealistic picture of beauty. The images and videos are often edited to remove imperfections. It's important to celebrate and embrace natural parts of your body, including cellulite, stretch marks, and acne.

- To improve your body image and self-esteem, avoid comparing yourself to others. Instead, focus on your own journey.

- Remember that you are worthy, powerful, and beautiful. By following the tips and strategies in this chapter, you can cultivate a positive body image and self-esteem.

In the next chapter, we will explore how to build positive relationships and manage the romantic feelings you may develop toward others as you get older.

PREPARING FOR THE FUTURE — HEALTHY RELATIONSHIPS AND ROMANTIC FEELINGS

As you grow up, you may begin to develop romantic feelings for others. These feelings can make you happy and excited but may be a little confusing at first. Understanding the difference between romantic and platonic feelings, how to set boundaries in a relationship, and the importance of communication are all crucial for a safe and positive experience when you enter the world of romantic relationships.

In this chapter, we will provide guidance on starting a safe and happy relationship when you feel ready. But first, let's explore romantic feelings and how they differ from other emotions.

Understanding Romantic Feelings: Navigating Crushes and First Loves

During puberty, your emotional state matures along with your body. One of the new feelings you may experience is that you may find yourself romantically interested in someone. Initially, you might not fully understand why you feel the way you do around them. Later, you will realize that your feelings for them differ from how you feel about your other friends.

You may notice different sensations, like butterflies in your stomach, a reddening of your face, or blushing when they are nearby. You might think about them often, wondering how they are and how they feel about you. These feelings are all completely normal. They are a sign that you have a crush on that person.

Having a crush is a natural experience, but it's important to treat the person respectfully and consider their feelings, as well. For example, they may not share your romantic interest. If they communicate that to you, you should respect their decision.

There's a difference between liking someone as a friend and having romantic feelings for them, and it's important to understand these differences. When you like someone as a friend, it's called a platonic relationship. In this case, you enjoy spending time with them, talking to them, and seeing them, but you don't have any romantic feelings towards them or see yourself being in a romantic relationship with them.

Regardless of your feelings for someone, you should respect their feelings and wishes. If someone has stated that they're not interested in you romantically, it's crucial not to pursue them further. Remember that you are a wonderful, beautiful, and strong individual deserving of a healthy relationship with someone who shares your feelings.

Finding someone who feels the same way about you may take time, but it will be worth the wait. When you find someone who likes you as much as you like them, you will have an entirely new challenge — navigating your first relationship.

Having your first relationship is an exciting but sometimes daunting experience. Your first relationship is something you will remember for a long time. However, there's no rush. In fact, you may not develop romantic feelings for someone until you are older.

When you enter a relationship, there are important factors to consider to ensure it is a safe and healthy relationship. Here are some of the most important ones.

Boundaries, Respect, and Consent

Being in a relationship comes with important points to consider, which determine whether it is a healthy relationship or not. When you start dating someone, it can be challenging to understand what is acceptable in the relationship. Above all, it is crucial that you feel safe and respected.

A healthy relationship is one in which both people respect boundaries and treat one another with respect. But what exactly are boundaries?

Boundaries are like lines that define what is okay and not okay in a relationship. Just as countries have borders, you also have personal boundaries. These are imaginary lines that you and your partner should not cross without proper permission. For example, when you begin dating, you might only feel comfortable holding hands and not ready to kiss. This is a boundary you have set.

Your partner will also have some boundaries, and it's essential to respect each other's boundaries and never pressure one another to do something you aren't comfortable with. It's always better to ask for consent before trying something new, especially if you're unsure about their comfort level.

Consent is the same as asking for permission. For example, before holding your partner's hand, ask, "Is it okay if I hold your hand?" If they say yes, that's great. But if they say no, respect their boundary, just as you would want them to respect yours. Remember, no means no, and you must never try to pressure your partner into anything they aren't comfortable with. Both of you should feel safe enough in the relationship to say no.

Saying no to someone doesn't mean you like them any less. It simply means that you aren't ready to do something. Building trust and taking things at your own pace is essential in any relationship, regardless of age. If your partner truly cares about you, they will respect your boundaries.

Healthy vs. Unhealthy Relationships

When you first start dating someone, it can be hard to tell if you are in a healthy or unhealthy relationship. Healthy relationships are great! They can improve your self-esteem, make you feel more confident, and make you happy. Signs of a healthy relationship include:

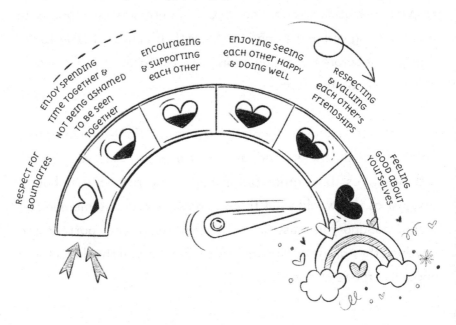

- Respect for each other's boundaries

- Enjoying spending time together and not being ashamed to be seen together

- Encouraging and supporting each other

- Enjoying seeing each other happy and doing well

- Respecting and valuing each other's friendships

- Feeling good about yourselves

In a healthy relationship, you have space to grow and mature at your own pace. This is especially important when you're still young and discovering who you are meant to be. If your partner doesn't give you room to grow and develop, it may indicate an unhealthy relationship. Signs of an unhealthy relationship include:

- Being mean to you in front of others or when you are alone

- Ignoring your boundaries or pressuring you into doing things you are uncomfortable with

- Putting you down, discouraging you, and pointing out your flaws and insecurities

- Lying to you

- Acting strangely or differently toward you in front of your friends

- Stopping you from spending time with your friends, isolating you, and talking negatively about your friends

- Not treating you with kindness and respect

If you notice any of these signs, you are likely not in a healthy relationship. In that case, the best thing to do is to end the relationship before someone gets hurt. Remember, you deserve to be with someone who loves and supports you. Don't settle for an unhealthy relationship, no matter how much you like the person.

Red Flags in a Relationship

You might have heard people talk about "red flags" in relationships. Red flags usually signify danger in the real world, and it's very much the same in relationships. Red flags indicate that something isn't quite right or may be unhealthy. Red flags include not respecting your partner's boundaries, treating them unkindly, and not giving them space to grow and spend time with their friends and family.

Seeing red flags doesn't always mean the person is bad; it might just mean they're not the right person for you.

In general, any relationship or person who does not respect your boundaries or makes you feel like anything less than the beautiful and unique person you are is a sign of an unhealthy relationship. Consider these red flags and end the relationship as soon as possible.

Staying in a relationship with someone despite your friends and family raising red flags, or noticing red flags yourself, is dangerous and will only lead to more heartbreak. Therefore, it's best to end the relationship gently before anyone gets hurt.

When you decide to end a relationship, it's important to respect your partner. Don't blame them for the relationship ending. Instead, treat them kindly and explain why you don't think it is the right time for the relationship, then give them the privacy and time they need to process the end of the relationship.

It is never easy to end a relationship. Still, it is best to do so when you realize the relationship isn't healthy or brings you more sadness than joy.

The Importance of Communication in Relationships

Communication is crucial in any relationship. Discussing your feelings with your partner and allowing them to share theirs can help build respect and trust, and foster a healthy relationship.

It isn't always easy to talk about the more serious aspects of a relationship, such as your expectations, boundaries, and things that upset you. Still, if you don't focus on clear communication, you or your partner might not even realize when you've hurt or upset each other.

In many cases, you can keep your relationship healthy just by communicating with each other. Check in with your partner to see how they are doing. Support them if they are stressed and remind them of what a wonderful person they are. Listen when they tell you about the things they don't like about the relationship. Just doing these simple things can help you maintain a healthy relationship.

During conversations about your relationship, remember the following:

· Stay calm and listen to your partner.

· Treat them with kindness and respect, even if you disagree.

- Avoid interrupting them when they are speaking.

- Explain your feelings without blame.

- Don't leave important things unsaid.

- Don't get angry or defensive when you disagree.

- Don't pressure your partner into doing something they aren't comfortable with.

- Never disregard your partner's feelings; they are important.

By maintaining open communication in a relationship, you can deal with problems as soon as they arise and ensure you and your partner are happy. Communicating and listening to each other will make you feel loved and appreciated, helping foster a healthy relationship.

Key Takeaways from Chapter 8

- It's normal to develop romantic feelings for someone as you enter puberty. These feelings are different than platonic relationships.

- Respect, boundaries, and asking for consent (permission) are crucial in any relationship. Remember, no means no.

- Recognizing red flags is essential to identify an unhealthy relationship.

- Communication is vital in relationships in order to maintain respect, trust, and a healthy dynamic.

It's important to remember that not everyone feels ready for a romantic relationship at the same time, and that's perfectly normal. You should never feel pressured to be in a relationship if you don't want one or haven't found someone you're interested in romantically.

You are unique and beautiful just as you are, and the right person will come into your life when the time is right. Embrace your individuality and continue to grow and explore the world around you. Trust that love will find its way to you when the time is right.

CONCLUSION

Congratulations on completing this book!

You've learned a lot about puberty and navigating the changes in your body. Puberty is an exciting and unique journey that signifies your transition from a child to an adult. Remember, everyone goes through puberty at their own pace, so don't worry if you start earlier or later than others.

During puberty, hormones play a significant role in causing the physical and emotional changes you experience. Your body will go through growth spurts, your shape will change, and you'll notice hair growth in new places. You'll also start having your period, which is a normal part of becoming a woman.

Breast development is another change that occurs during puberty. If you feel the need, you might consider buying your first bra. There are different types of bras available, so finding the right size and style is essential for comfort and support.

Taking care of your body becomes more important during puberty. Establishing a personal care routine, including regular showers, using deodorant, and practicing good oral hygiene, will keep you clean and healthy. Remember the importance of exercise, staying hydrated, getting enough sleep, and maintaining a healthy diet.

Friendships may change as you grow older, and that's normal. Focus on being a good friend and surrounding yourself with friends who support and encourage you. It's better to have a few close friends than lots of acquaintances.

Mood swings are common due to hormonal changes, especially before and during your period. Understanding the causes of your emotions can help you manage them. Taking care of yourself by getting enough sleep, spending time in the sun, and managing stress can help stabilize your mood.

Body image and self-esteem can also be affected during puberty. Remember that your body is unique and beautiful, just the way it is. Avoid comparing yourself to others and focus on embracing your individuality.

Finally, as you enter puberty, you may develop romantic feelings for others. It's important to enjoy yourself, respect boundaries, ask for consent, and communicate openly in any relationship. Remember, you are in control of your own body and choices.

Embrace your journey, celebrate yourself, and use the knowledge you've gained to guide you. Remember, you are a beautiful girl, and you are growing into a strong and amazing woman.

As you continue your path through puberty, support and encourage your friends, too. Each of you is unique, and everyone's puberty journey happens at their own pace — but deep down, what's happening inside your bodies is the same. You're not alone in this journey, as billions of women have gone through what you're experiencing and stand beside you.

"Do not live someone else's life and someone else's idea of womanhood. Womanhood is you. Womanhood is everything that is inside of you."
*~ **Viola Davis***

You are unique, you are beautiful, and you are ready to conquer the world.

BEMBERTON
BOOKS

THANKS

FOR READING MY

BOOK!

I appreciate you picking this guide to help your tween girl understand and navigate the exciting yet sometimes puzzling journey of puberty.

I would be so grateful if you could take a moment to leave an honest review or a star rating on Amazon.
(A star rating is just a couple of clicks away.)

By leaving a review, you'll help other parents discover this valuable resource for their own children. Thank you!

To leave a review & help spread the word

SCAN
HERE

REFERENCES

1. *Body image.* (n.d.). National Eating Disorders Collaboration. https://nedc.com.au/eating-disorders/eating-disorders-explained/body-image/

2. Breehl, L., & Caban, O. (2023). *Physiology, puberty.* StatPearls Publishing.

3. Byzak, A. (2018, August 20). *5 ways the sun impacts your mental and physical health.* Tri-City Medical Center. https://www.tricitymed.org/2018/08/5-ways-the-sun-impacts-your-mental-and-physical-health

4. *Cellulite.* (2021, October 28). Cleveland Clinic. https://my.clevelandclinic.org/health/diseases/17694-cellulite

5. Cherry, K. (2022, November 7). *What is self-esteem?* Verywell Mind. https://www.verywellmind.com/what-is-self-esteem-2795868

6. *Everything you wanted to know about puberty.* (n.d.). Nemours Teens Health. https://kidshealth.org/en/teens/puberty.html

7. *55+ Strong Women Quotes to Inspire You* (2019, April 2). Shutterfly. https://www.shutterfly.com/ideas/strong-women-quotes/

8. Greep, M. (2022, February 2). *How the 'perfect body' has changed throughout the decades.* Mail Online. https://www.dailymail.co.uk/femail/article-10467643/How-perfect-body-changed-decades.html

9. *Growth spurts & baby growth spurts.* (2021, November 19). Cleveland Clinic. https://my.clevelandclinic.org/health/diseases/22070-growth-spurts

10. *Heavy menstrual bleeding.* (2022, August 17). Centers for Disease Control and Prevention. https://www.cdc.gov/ncbddd/blooddisorders/women/menorrhagia.html

11. Holland, K. (2019, December 5). *What causes extreme mood shifts in women.* Healthline. https://www.healthline.com/health/mood-swings-in-women

12. Jitesh, A., Chaabna, K., Doraiswamy, S., & Cheema, S. (2021, May 18). *Importance of sleep for teenagers.* Weill Cornell Medicine—Qatar. https://qatar-weill.cornell.edu/institute-for-population-health/community/stay-safe-stay-healthy/issue/importance-of-sleep-for-teenagers

13. Mandal, A. (2022, December 6). *What are hormones?* News Medical. https://www.news-medical.net/health/What-are-Hormones.aspx

14. Makvana, H. (2023, June 1). *10 important conflict resolution skills for teenagers.* Mom Junction. https://www.momjunction.com/articles/important-conflict-resolution-skills-for-teenagers_00106119/

15. McCallum, K. (2021, September 24). *Menstrual cramps: 5 tips for getting relief from period pain.* Houston Methodist. https://www.houstonmethodist.org/blog/articles/2021/sep/menstrual-cramps-5-tips-for-getting-relief-from-period-pain/

16. *Menstrual cycle.* (2022, June 9). Better Health Channel. https://www.betterhealth.vic.gov.au/health/conditionsandtreatments/menstrual-cycle

17. *Puberty.* (n.d.). Planned Parenthood. https://www.plannedparenthood.org/learn/teens/puberty

18. Sheehan, J. (2010, February 17). *Mood swings: PMS and your emotional health.* Everyday Health. https://www.everydayhealth.com/pms/mood-swings

19. Tallman Smith, S. (2017, November 14). *How to manage mood swings naturally.* Everyday Health. https://www.everydayhealth.com/emotional-health/how-manage-mood-swings-naturally

20. *10 tips for improving your self-esteem.* (n.d.). Reachout. https://au.reachout.com/articles/10-tips-for-improving-your-self-esteem

21. *The first bra guide: how and when to buy your daughter a bra.* (2019, May 17). Lingerie Outlet Store. https://lingerieoutletstore.co.uk/magazine/the-first-bra-guide-how-and-when-to-buy-your-daughter-a-bra/

22. Watson, S. (2019, March 8). *How to deal with premenstrual mood swings.* Healthline. https://www.healthline.com/health/pms-mood-swings

Made in the USA
Coppell, TX
31 October 2023